101

Business Travelers Do To Sabotage Success

Harry Knitter

Richard Chang Associates, Inc.
Publications Division
Irvine, California

101 Stupid Things Business Travelers Do To Sabotage Success

Harry Knitter

Library of Congress Catalog Card Number
97-69477

© 1998, Richard Chang Associates, Inc.
Printed in the United States of America

ISBN 1-883553-98-9

Editors:	Bill Foster and Karen Johnson
Reviewers:	Shirley Codrey and Richard Baisner
Graphic Layout:	Christina Slater
Cover Design:	Dena Putnam

Richard Chang Associates, Inc.
Publications Division
15265 Alton Parkway, Suite 300
Irvine, CA 92618
(800) 756-8096   (949) 727-7477
Fax: (949) 727-7007
www.richardchangassociates.com

RICHARD
CHANG
ASSOCIATES

About The Author

Harry Knitter is a million-mile traveler who has personally performed or witnessed many stupid things done by *Business Travelers To Sabotage Success*. As an executive with Chrysler Marine in the 1970's, he frequently visited Europe in the development of a European advertising program. He has also traveled extensively in Europe for his current employer.

Harry has been a successful marketing director for over 30 years. He is a two-time winner of the American Management Association's Effie Award for marketing productivity; and a four-time winner of first prize in worldwide competition conducted annually by Floraprint, International, a horticultural marketing organization.

He has published two travel guidebooks, *Holding Pattern: Airport Waiting Made Easy*, a book that makes time fly when the plane doesn't; and *Why You Should Take Your Travel Agent to Lunch*, "the book to read before you book." His third book, *A Sweet Sampling of Floral Delights*, includes original prose and poetry on flowers.

Acknowledgments

I am pleased to share my experience and knowledge in the area of business travel, since I have spent thousands of hours on the road during my 38-year business career. As I organized the material for this book, I received support and encouragement from several sources. In particular, Jerry Jenkins and his associates at The Jenkins Group have been terrific supporters of my writing habit, though they try to talk me out of it occasionally.

I am grateful for the invaluable help that my wife, Nancy, provided to ensure that I met the deadlines for this project.

And I especially appreciate the contributions of Bill Foster and the folks from Richard Chang Associates, Inc. who sought me out and invited me to participate in this effort.

Table of Contents

3. You've Arrived! 29

4. It's Showtime! 49

5. Health Is Wealth............................. 67

6. Now You Become The Foreigner........ 75

Introduction

"Fear or stupidity has always been the basis
of most human actions."

—Albert Einstein

Many people who don't travel on business think that life on the road would typically be glorious, glamorous, and exciting. But those who live their business lives on the road often experience tension, anxiety, loneliness, fatigue, and boredom.

For someone who's based at the home office, however, business travel can represent an oasis—a needed break from the routine—some time away from the clutches of the boss, away from boring meetings, and some welcome distance from that huge stack of paperwork that's clogging your IN basket. Then again, life on the road can present the inexperienced traveler with a myriad of new and stupid adventures.

Prepare For Pressure

Ideally, things go smoothly back at the office while you're on the road. But if they don't, prepare yourself for added pressure while you're trying to achieve your objectives during your trip. And, unless you have an assistant who can handle your office duties while you're gone, prepare to face that challenging "catch-up" period that will keep you occupied for days after you return.

Veteran travelers tend to take travel challenges in stride better than inexperienced road warriors. As you climb the organizational chart, you'll have more people to support you and make sure that the important issues are dealt with in your absence. Also, your trip agenda will usually keep you away from the nitty-gritty and allow you to focus on the big picture.

It's Best To Be Road Wise

The seasoned pros know that there is a variety of ways to avoid doing stupid things that preclude or delay the achievement of objectives. Some are simple and obvious, while others are more difficult to identify. But once you recognize and avoid them, you are almost guaranteed success in your travels.

Chapter 1

Pre-Trip Prep

#1 Do You Really Have To Go?

You bolt out the door anytime your customer snaps his fingers. You don't give a hoot how much the trip costs—you just want him to look into your bloodshot eyes and give you the order. You can't do that over the phone. Of course, sometimes he looks into your bloodshot eyes and proceeds to tell you "No!"

What's Wrong?

→ Giving the personal touch does not always makes you better than your competition.

→ When you're on the road, your other accounts suffer because you're the only one who knows what's going on.

→ Mr. Bigdome likes to be taken to lunch so he can tell you about his son's antique skateboard collection. You always oblige.

→ You've never bothered to involve your staff in client contact.

Some Success Strategies:

Look at the potential return on your investment of time and money. Compare the possible impact of a phone conversation or conference call involving the customer and selected members of your team. Then look at the costs for each, and put a value on the time you'll waste in airports, circling the destination, etc. See if you can coax the client into coming to your office instead, or look into video conferencing. If it still makes sense to fly to the client location, bon voyage!

#2 Hello, Quasi Airlines? Get Me Someplace Fast!

You always book flights directly with the airlines, figuring it's smart to eliminate the middleman. And you're not a travel agent!

What's Wrong?

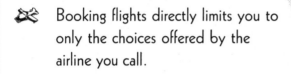

-  Booking flights directly limits you to only the choices offered by the airline you call.

- You have too much time on your hands.

- You're unaware that a good travel agent can actually save you money.

- Getting frequent flyer miles is often the motivating factor in the choice of airlines.

- You miss out on additional savings when the fare drops one week after you booked the flight and you weren't aware of the price cut.

Some Success Strategies:

Check your Yellow Pages for a reputable travel agent. Or ask around the office, the micro-brew dispensing machine, or while you're waiting for a flu shot. Ask people who they'd recommend outside of their brother-in-law. Select the one that suits your needs and start working with them as soon as possible so they can analyze your needs and develop a cost-efficient plan. Most services are provided at no cost, since the agent receives commissions from airlines and hotels.

#3 You Paid That Much, Stupid?

The Smart Alec in the next seat on your flight shows you his ticket, and you notice that his fare was 50 percent less than what you paid. He laughs uncontrollably when you tell him how much your ticket cost.

What's Wrong?

💰 You always wait until the last minute to book your flights.

💰 You book directly with your favorite airline, figuring that gives you greater control.

💰 You don't like people giving you advice—especially those smartypants travel agents.

💰 With what you paid in airfares last year, you could have bought your own private jet.

Some Success Strategies:

By working with a professional travel agent, you get a wide range of options on available flights to your destination. And since there are 60,000 fare changes every day, they are better-equipped to find the best deals. In addition, they'll track reductions prior to departure and cut costs even more! Be sure to book your flights as early as possible and consider a Saturday night stayover to cut your costs.

#4 Hang The Cost, Gimme Those Miles!

Your employees like to make their own travel reservations. They often book flights that suit their own needs and not the organization's. You discovered that one employee flew to four extra cities just to earn extra airline miles and another took the scenic route by train.

What's Wrong?

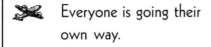 Everyone is going their own way.

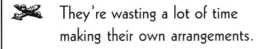 They're wasting a lot of time making their own arrangements.

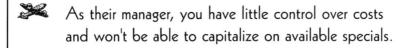 As their manager, you have little control over costs and won't be able to capitalize on available specials.

 They'll avoid Saturday stayovers and the company will wind up paying through the nose.

Some Success Strategies:

By appointing a competent travel agent to do the booking, you'll be in control and the organization will save suitcases of money. For example, by enrolling eligible staff members in AARP and AAA, many hotels will discount their rates up to 20 percent. In addition, you'll have consistent travel records for future analysis. Your employees may get less miles, but your organization will save a bundle.

#5 Make A List
And Check It Twice

You find yourself forgetting things every time you travel. It's annoying, embarrassing, and costly.

What's Wrong?

☑ You wind up with the wrong things in the wrong place at the wrong time.

☑ You have to repurchase items left behind once you arrive.

☑ You're known to customers as Sam the Scramblin' Man.

☑ Business travel makes you listless!

Some Success Strategies:

Standardize your preparations. Keep a separate toiletry kit so you don't have to start from scratch every time out. Use the same luggage so that you develop a routine and don't vary preparations from trip to trip. As soon as you know you're going on the road, start building a checklist of "must-haves" and don't forget to review the checklist before you depart. If organization is not your forte', have your secretary prepare your itinerary and luggage for you.

#6 Don't Leave Home Without An Itinerary

You're heading for China for three weeks. First, the travel agent needs your passport and credit card numbers. Then, you need your seat numbers, etc., etc. There are so many numbers to keep track of, your head is spinning. You're a basket case already, and you haven't even left the terminal.

What's Wrong?

\#   You rely on your memory for most common numbers in your life.

\#   Your memory isn't what it used to be.

\#   With all the baggage you're taking along, it's difficult to find your ticket wallet, your passport holder, and your boarding passes.

\#   You haven't prepared well for this trip.

Some Success Strategies:

Whether you're jumping out of town for a weekend convention or heading to China for three weeks, you'll be asked for your tickets, your passport, your seat assignments, your luggage tag code numbers, your rental car i.d. number, and your hotel confirmation numbers at various times along the way. Ask your travel agent to put together a daily itinerary for you to follow, with all available information in one place. Keep your credit cards and travelers' checks in one billfold.

#7 Peter Piper Packed A Peck Of Potent Pills

Peter Piper made a big mistake when he packed his pills in his checked baggage. Naturally, Murphy's Law of travel says that your bag with the medicine will be the first one lost. Now, you are in need of your medication.

What's Wrong?

- You can't function normally without the medication.

- You forgot to pack a backup supply.

- There's no time to get a shipment from home.

- The pharmacy won't give you pills without prescriptions.

- Some pills make you bigger, and some pills make you small. But, the ones you forgot won't do anything at all.

Some Success Strategies:

Always keep your medications close to you and within easy reach. Also, keep a copy of your prescriptions so you can refill them in a distant town if necessary. Keep your doctor's phone numbers with you just in case. Don't ever take chances by checking luggage containing your medications. Instead, let people nearby call you "Peter, Peter, proper pill and pumpkin eater."

#8 You Brought Everything But The Moths

Like many travelers, you take far too many clothes on every trip and wind up carrying them instead of wearing them. When you bring most of your closet along, it feels like your arms stretch a couple of inches on every trip.

What's Wrong?

- Hotel porters are getting rich on your hefty tips.

- You don't spend much time planning what to take. As a result, your combinations are mixed but not matched.

- Your clothes are wrinkled before you wear them and you'll need to have them pressed at about five dollars per garment.

- You risk getting a back injury.

Some Success Strategies:

Once the length of stay and content of your travels are determined, you can begin to lay out outfits that will coordinate with each other, so you don't have to bring your entire wardrobe. Take clothing and shoes that can be switched around for a new look each day, without extra sets needed to keep you looking sharp! For example, different colored blazers and two or three sets of non-wrinkling slacks are a good starting combo for men.

#9 Your Desk Is Clean, But Your Briefcase Is Bulging

Large stacks of correspondence are swept into the briefcase before you leave on a trip. You figure you'll have plenty of time on the road to catch up on your paperwork.

What's Wrong?

🗂 With noise and distractions taking place around you, it's not that easy to get work done.

🗂 You're too ambitious and unrealistic. Work on the road is not as easy as it may appear to be.

🗂 You're preoccupied with the stack of work waiting for you in your hotel room.

🗂 The paperwork you brought along doesn't seem as important as trying out the hotel tennis court.

Some Success Strategies:

The most important business to attend to while on the road is the business at hand—not what your brought from home. Be realistic about your workload. Allow yourself some time to relax and enjoy the surroundings when you go on a trip. Don't try to fill up every waking moment with business activity. Include time in your agenda for delays, disasters, and the meeting that runs overtime. Stop and smell the roses.

Chapter 2

We're On Our Way

#10 No Assigned Seat? Sorry. . .

You were extra-busy when you made flight reservations and now you discover you neglected to get a seat assignment. Guess what? The plane is full and you get the last seat in the last row—in the middle!

What's Wrong?

☹ You have no elbow room.

☹ So much for your intention to get work done en route.

☹ It'll take you weeks to exit the plane.

☹ The crew runs out of meals by the time they reach your row.

☹ You find yourself book-ended by twin Sumo wrestlers.

☹ The Sumos are ready to rumble.

Some Success Strategies:

Always ask for seat assignments when you book your flights. If you work with a travel agent, they'll keep a file of your location preferences and handle seat assignments routinely. Sitting in the exit door row is a good idea because it provides you with more leg room. If something like this does happen, consider volunteering to give up your seat and flying on the next available flight. You may get a voucher for several hundred dollars in return for your gratuitous move.

#11 What Do You Mean I'm Too Early To Check In?

Every other week, you've taken the same flight from the same airport to the same destination to work for the same client. Heck, you even sit in the same seat. It's become so routine, you don't bother checking your tickets anymore. Now, unbeknownst to you, the airline changed their flight schedule and the 7:30 flight no longer exists, so your travel coordinator booked you on the 12:30.

What's Wrong

- You're in for a long wait.

- Your travel coordinator needs some coaching regarding her communication skills.

- Arriving at your destination on time is now impossible.

- Checking in five hours early is stupid.

- It could be worse. At least the departure time wasn't changed to 6:30 (meaning you missed your flight).

Some Success Strategies:

Always check your tickets and itinerary as soon as you get them. Make sure your flight is going to the right city on the right day at the right time. Airline schedules tend to change as frequently as the weather in Minnesota. Never assume your travel agent or coordinator will inform you of schedule changes ahead of time. And, if you do arrive five hours early, be creative with your time—shop, eat, sleep, read, get some work done, make phone calls, people-watch, write a letter to your mother, etc.

#12 A Recipe For Cooked Goose

You were greeted with a delay announcement when you checked in, so you decide to quaff a few beers. By the time your flight took off, you were well-sloshed. On board, you became obnoxious and an unruly jerk. The crew asked you to settle down, but you insisted on giving them reasons to take action.

What's Wrong?

 You're unaware that airline crews receive special training to deal with morons like you.

 You think you can raise a ruckus without being held accountable.

 The captain is thinking about dropping you off at the nearest exit—without a parachute.

 Other passengers are requesting seat changes.

 You could be on your way to jail for weeks or months.

Some Success Strategies:

You need to take positive action to avoid serious consequences of your stupid behavior. Apologize profusely and return to your seat quietly and without further threatening action. Try sleeping it off. Always keep in mind that alcohol has more "kick" in a pressurized environment like an airline cabin.

#13 Prepared For
A Double Feature?

You get on the plane carrying about a week's supply of crackers, dip, and chips to help pass the time while en route. In the process of munching your goodies, you get crumbs all over your neighbor's clothes, your seat, and the floor surrounding you.

What's Wrong?

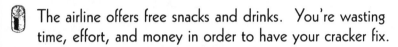 The airline offers free snacks and drinks. You're wasting time, effort, and money in order to have your cracker fix.

The flight attendant might ask you to share your goodies with your fellow passengers.

The crumbs and soft drink stains you get all over your seat-mate don't increase his limited capacity to smile.

You've made a general nuisance of yourself. You are not exactly demonstrating professionalism.

Some Success Strategies:

Make sure you schedule a meal before you go to the airport. This will help curb your hunger pangs. You should act like a professional whenever you're traveling on business. It's not a time to demonstrate immature or boorish behavior. When you're in the presence of your peers, look, act, and behave like a leader. And someday you may be one.

#14 I'm Happy To Be Herezzxqmrtxseeescxz!

You planned to write an important speech on the plane, but just as the script begins to take shape, your computer battery ran out of juice. Not only do you have to start over, your laptop won't even boot.

What's Wrong?

- You failed to recharge the battery before you departed.

- You don't have access to an outlet that can run your computer with the converter.

- That's OK, because you don't have a converter with you anyway.

- Instead, you'll have to watch the in-flight movie. Too bad it's in French.

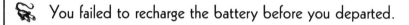

Some Success Strategies:

Check with the crew on your plane and ask them if the galley has electrical outlets that can be used for recharging, if you can find your converter. If you are using your computer while in the boarding lounge, plug it in then instead of using your battery. In the future, some airliners will be equipped with plugs you can use near your seat to recharge the batteries. It will be in first and business class only at first, but may eventually make it back to economy.

#15 You Kids Are Driving Me Nuts!

You brought along a pile of work that you must finish before you arrive at your destination. But conditions on a flight can't be controlled, and you're seated between two obnoxious teenagers who've started a peanut war.

What's Wrong?

- You're having great difficulty concentrating, much less getting any work done.

- You should have finished your administrative work before you left.

- The teenagers are referring to you as "the enemy target."

- Fellow passengers have little empathy for your dilemma.

- It's too late to upgrade to first class.

Some Success Strategies:

Ask the flight attendant if there might be a quiet open seat somewhere in the cabin. Tell her the importance of your project, and she might move you back in the cabin or up to first class. If not, ask to borrow a pair of earplugs. If you can't finish now, you'll just have to do it after your plane lands. Learn from the experience, and travel first class next time.

#16 Leave A Paper Trail

You've got your tickets, your passport, your itinerary, and your
meeting notes all conveniently packed into your briefcase.
Unfortunately, your briefcase is gone and nowhere to be found.

What's Wrong?

✔ You don't have back-up copies.

✔ Someone else is taking your
flight to Hong Kong.

✔ You were careless with your
belongings.

✔ The meeting will be a total
loss without your notes.

Some Success Strategies:

Make duplicate copies of your tickets, passport, itinerary, and
anything else that's important to the success of the trip. They're easier
to replace when you have copies. Keep the copies in a separate
location from the originals. Leave copies with your secretary and a
family member or friend as well, so they know where you are, and how
to reach you.

#17 I Deplaned. . . Now Where Is De Plane?

You're on your way to New York and the plane stops in Pittsburgh. You get off to make a few phone calls and find yourself involved in a long conversation. The plane leaves and you're still gabbing on the phone. Your files, your clothes, and your laptop are on their way to New York, unaccompanied.

What's Wrong?

✈ You didn't pay attention to the scheduled departure time.

✈ You left your valuable computer unattended.

✈ You forgot to let the crew know that you were getting off to hit the phones.

✈ If you're lucky, you'll only lose a half day of work because of this faux-pas.

Some Success Strategies:

You've learned the hard way that you never leave your property, (especially your expensive computer) unattended while traveling. Since you've committed the mistake, contact the airline immediately and request their help in securing your stuff at the other end—that is, if it isn't already adopted by someone else. Next time when you need to make a phone call, consider using a phone on the plane.

#18 So, You've Been To The Army Surplus Store?

You're waiting with a group of your associates for the luggage to come bouncing down the chute in the baggage claim area. Your bags arrive, and they look like you salvaged them from your WW II buddies.

What's Wrong?

 Ragged luggage tatters your image.

 You appear to be a cheapskate.

 You haven't kept up with the times.

 Your bags are just as likely to fall apart as they are to get lost.

 Your associates never figured you as a guerilla rebel.

Some Success Strategies:

Get a quality set of luggage (with wheels, please) early in your career and stick with it. Developing a set routine is one of the basics of smooth traveling, since it precludes the necessity for reinventing the wheel every time you go on the road. Get advice from some of your frequent flying friends about what type of luggage works best for them. Remember, if a gorilla can break it, it isn't worth buying. If you're in the Marine Corps, you can keep using the camouflage bags.

#19 No Time To Do Things Right

You don't review the trip files your assistant hands you as you hurry out the door. Arriving in Washington D.C., you discover that you have your colleague's speech on the latest trends in the gaming industry, and he has yours in Las Vegas covering sexual harassment.

What's Wrong?

📁 Not checking your files before you leave is a gamble.

📁 Blaming your assistant is a cop-out. You are to blame for this dilemma. Besides, she's the boss' niece.

📁 Since you're terrible at ad-libbing, you're sunk.

📁 Your colleague isn't exactly ecstatic in Sin City.

Some Success Strategies:

This problem won't occur if you review your trip materials before you depart. To solve the immediate crisis, contact your host and request a delay in the delivery of your presentation until you have the correct script and visual support. If that doesn't work, try to reconstruct the presentation on-site. After all, you are the expert—although a disorganized one at best.

#20 Don't Go Bonkers In Airports

Your flight is canceled and you pound on the gate agent's desk and demand action. Every vein in your neck bulges out as you give everyone a piece of your mind. Despite your tantrum, the flight is still canceled.

What's Wrong?

🌸 Loss of composure is a childish reaction.

🌸 You feel totally out of control . . . and you are.

🌸 The gate agent has no power to solve the problem.

🌸 You're embarrassing yourself without even realizing it.

🌸 You're faced with an unplanned overnight stay.

Some Success Strategies:

Call your travel agent and solicit his help in solving your dilemma. Airline personnel are not to blame for most delays and are generally powerless to solve problems that involve maintenance and parts. Be happy they're not taking off with a defective piece of equipment. Take out your aggressions by filling out a customer complaint form. No one will read it, but you'll feel better anyway.

#21 Pittsburgh To L.A. And Back In A Day? No Way!

You try to restrict most of your travel to day trips. That means you take off at the crack of dawn and return home in the wee hours of the morning. Then you attempt to go into the office the next day.

What's Wrong?

- You think you're saving money, but you're absorbing a lot of wear and tear.

- Your saved funds will all be spent on doctor bills.

- Your mind is subjected to a lot more stress when traveling than you realize.

- The whole day is spent looking out of a plane window.

Some Success Strategies:

You need to reassess your priorities and come to the realization that the jet age is working against you. Take some time to look at life realistically and find out what you want to do to build for the future. If daily cross-country flights are glamorous and exciting, you'll soon find out they can also be nerve-wracking and frustrating. Consider taking red-eye flights more often if you find it easy to sleep on the plane.

#22 Passport? Check. Visa? Check. Tickets? Check. Currency? Uh Oh!

You've planned every detail of your trip overseas very carefully. You're sure that everything you need for a successful international trip is in order. You confidently arrive at your destination only to find that it's the middle of the night and the currency exchange kiosks are closed until morning.

What's Wrong

 With no local currency, your ability to secure transportation to you hotel is reduced significantly.

 If you're hungry, you won't be able to buy anything to eat.

 Leaving home without them makes no cents.

 The exchange rate is as foreign to you as the country itself.

Some Success Strategies:

When traveling to another country that has it's own currency, it's a good idea to exchange your currency before you arrive. This way, you won't be forced to barter your watch for a cab ride to the hotel. Also, you may be able to receive a more favorable exchange rate from your own local bank. The fees and commissions charged by some airport currency exchanges are very high. And, even if they are open, you'll often find yourself waiting in a long line, which is never any fun after a long flight.

Chapter 3

You've Arrived!

#23 When Airlines Don't Follow Suit

The airline got you to your destination on schedule, but your luggage is nowhere to be found. You file a report, but the missing luggage contains your dress clothes. In the morning, you're supposed to represent your company at the big trade show.

What's Wrong?

 The only clothes you have are those you're wearing and they're crumpled, wrinkled, and smelly.

 All the clothing stores are shut down for the night.

 The airline tracked down your bag—it's in Bora-Bora.

 The good news? It'll be here next week!

 You'll be the only one at the trade show wearing shorts and a sweat shirt from your alma mater.

Some Success Strategies:

Always carry on your dress clothes and your toiletry kit. For now, ask the front desk or restaurant manager if they can loan you a jacket. Trusting that the airline would get your crucial piece of lost luggage to you is like telling your teenage son that he should fill up the tank of your car when he has time. It'll never happen the way you want it to.

#24 You Don't Have Time For A Morning Shower

You have to skip your usual shower because the hotel's hot water supply ran out. It turns out to be a hot and humid day and you're soaked with perspiration. You're more than fragrant to those around you.

What's Wrong?

 Getting up early is not one of your strong suits.

 Considering that they're wool, you brought the wrong suits.

 By mid-afternoon, your fragrance is much like Eau de Goat.

 You wonder why your hosts are cutting your meetings short.

Some Success Strategies:

When you're on the road, it's always a good idea to get up a bit earlier than everyone else, so you can shower and dress for breakfast on a relaxed schedule. The best thing you can do without a shower is spray-on and roll-on. And next time, bring suits that are better suited to warm temperatures. Consider taking a cold shower. It shouldn't take too long. Brrr.

#25 I Thought *You* Reserved The Car!

Nobody made a reservation and now you're stuck with a RentaBeetle. Your baggage hardly fits, and there's even less room for passengers.

What's Wrong?

↘ You're in for a long day.

↘ You didn't verify that your colleagues reserved a car.

↘ Murphy's Law says that when you forget, they automatically sell out. But when you remember, they have cars up to their pluckin' ukuleles.

↘ Your car may be little, but it's also expensive.

↘ Without reservations, you waste time filling out paperwork and forms.

↘ Stupid errors like this can drive you nuts.

Some Success Strategies:

Have your travel agent negotiate the best deal. And don't forget to give your frequent flyer number so you'll earn miles on your rental car usage. Most rental car companies keep customer profiles on file to minimize paperwork when you check out a car. Make sure you reserve the size of car suitable for your needs.

#26 Don't Be Taken
For A Ride

This is your first visit to this particular town and you're unfamiliar with this locale. So you jump in the cab and hand the driver the address. Ninety minutes later you're still circling the town and the meter has blown a fuse.

What's Wrong?

+ Cabbies' goal: Drain your billfold dry.

+ You run up a tab that's going to be tough to explain on your expense report.

+ You find yourself worrying about the cab ride instead of focusing on your business appointment.

+ If you wanted to take a tour, you would have signed up for one with your travel agent.

Some Success Strategies:

A hotel limo or van is generally more cost-effective, when the driver's only intent is getting you to the accurate address. As soon as you notice the roundabout route the cabbie is taking, tell him you were once a mapmaker and helped to design the street configuration in the town he's now using to pad your bill. Another protective device: Agree on a set price up front.

#27 But I Just Rented This...

You show up for an appointment at a General Motors plant in a Ford Taurus and find yourself blocked from entering the vendors' parking lot. Then you notice that all the other cars in the lot are GM automobiles.

What's Wrong?

✗ Using the competitors' products is a no-no whenever you're visiting the client's offices or plants.

✗ It's time for lunch, and you wind up driving. You're embarrassed when they tease you about your choice of rental cars.

✗ It's too late to change models in midstream on this trip.

✗ Life on the road would be much easier if you knew about these pitfalls in advance.

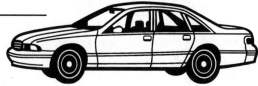

Some Success Strategies:

It's a good idea to be ultra-sensitive about the use of competitive products, no matter who you might be calling on. By using Brand X, you're demonstrating a lack of respect for the product line your hosts represent. In fact, you should try to use the products of your prospect or client whenever possible.

#28 I Thought *You* Were Doing The Agenda

You were so busy finalizing your trip itinerary, you failed to prepare a detailed meeting agenda. Without a reasonably tight agenda, your meeting is like a sailboat without sails. It still moves along, sluggishly, but never gets to the finish line.

What's Wrong?

⚓ Most people drift off the main subject frequently and never get back on course.

⚓ The rest of the participants are bored and disgusted.

⚓ Some people walk out before the meeting is over.

⚓ At the end, you're not sure you accomplished anything.

⚓ You've wasted valuable travel dollars.

Some Success Strategies:

Take a course in meeting management and pass around the materials and notes to everyone you meet with on a regular basis. Make sure everyone is prepared to contribute constructively. Don't make fun of any ideas expressed. Get rid of those who interrupt, disrupt, and erupt. You don't need them (unless one of them is your boss).

#29 Was I Supposed To Call You This Morning?

The hotel operator was asleep at the switch when you requested a wake-up call. None came, and now you're running late for a very important engagement.

What's Wrong?

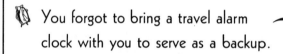 You forgot to bring a travel alarm clock with you to serve as a backup.

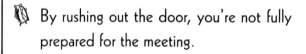 By rushing out the door, you're not fully prepared for the meeting.

🕭 Now you're late and are jeopardizing making a good impression.

🕭 Just your luck, the client happens to be a stickler for on-time performance.

🕭 The late start to your day may be a bad omen.

Some Success Strategies:

First, find a reliable alarm clock and carry it with you on all trips. Second, get to bed early the night before a big meeting on the road. Third, be consistently on time, so that if you should slip, it'll be perceived as a rare occasion and easily excused. Remember to adjust your clock when changing time zones.

#30 Without Business Cards, It's Tough To Do Business

When you're at a trade show, it's almost impossible to conduct business without your basic tools. Yet, here you are at the Ball Peen Hammer Exposition, and your assistant forgot to pack order forms and business cards.

What's Wrong?

- You should have gone over the checklist with him before you left the office.

- There's no time to have a supply shipped via overnight.

- It's tacky to write your name and title on co-worker's cards.

- You forgot to put extra cards in your brief case.

- Your prospects will think you're too unprofessional to conduct business with.

Some Success Strategies:

If you have access to a computer, try creating your own cards. Or, check the Yellow Pages and locate an all-night print shop. Have them make up a temporary supply while your assistant ships your regular cards and order forms. Be sure you set up a system to prevent this problem from happening in the future.

#31 Good Manners Count For Extra Credit

Your client invites you to his home for dinner with his family. You accept, then fail to bring a gift, and after the event, fail to express appreciation. You drink too much and tell tasteless stories.

What's Wrong?

- The client's wife thinks you're a thoughtless lout.

- You are a thoughtless lout.

- You let the pressure of business get in the way of good manners.

- You'll never be invited back for an encore.

- The client's wife could have been an enthusiastic ally; now she's ready to cut your image into confetti for your exit party.

Some Success Strategies:

Never show up at your client's home without an appropriate gift (don't bring a "how-to" cookbook). Be on your best behavior and demonstrate that you are a thoughtful, considerate person. After the event, send flowers and/or a nicely-written note of appreciation.

#32 Your Motto: Shopping Is My Bag

You're a souvenir fanatic. So much so that at every stop along your travel itinerary, you spend a month's salary on gifts and gadgets.

What's Wrong?

🎁 You find out too late that the stores' return policies are cast in bronze and you're stuck with stuff you don't need.

🎁 You also don't have time to run around to all the stores and argue about returning the merchandise.

🎁 In order to transport all of the gifts and gadgets home, you need an additional suitcase.

🎁 Your gift-buying snafu is absorbing so much of your attention, you're not accomplishing the business objectives you need to achieve before you head back home.

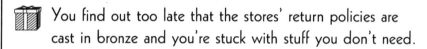

Some Success Strategies:

You're bound to be faced with dozens of distractions that influence your ability to complete the work that prompted the trip in the first place. Therefore, you will have to discipline yourself to concentrate on those activities that will contribute to the realization of your goals. Everything else is secondary—except for your most important activity, keeping your family at the top of you priority gift list. Ship gifts back home to avoid lugging them around.

#33 Guess What, Inspector?

Everything goes smoothly at the start of your trip until you get seated on the plane. Then the captain comes on the intercom system and announces that an FAA inspector has joined the crew in the cockpit while they prepare to take you and the rest of the passengers to Chicago. Unfortunately, he found out the young co-pilot left his license on the kitchen table back home. You aren't going anywhere.

What's Wrong?

📖 You've now encountered one of the many stupid things you'll experience during your career when you travel.

📖 The co-pilot has some explaining to do.
But that will not help you get to Chicago any faster.

📖 You're helpless, and your timing on the first leg of your trip is hopeless.

📖 You didn't bring anything to read or work on while you're on board.
And man, are you bored.

Some Success Strategies:

Never go anywhere without being prepared to wait at some point during your travel itinerary. A snafu in your arrangements is inevitable, and you may as well face it with finesse and a positive attitude. Buy a copy of *Holding Pattern: Airport Waiting Made Easy* at the airport gift shop or book store. You'll discover many creative tips on how to pass the time in an airport. Otherwise, consider transferring to another flight.

#34 Loose Lips Sink Relationships

You're invited by the biggest client on your roster to attend an off-site strategy meeting. Two days later, after you return home, a story in your local paper includes information that was discussed confidentially in the meeting. Your client receives a clip of the article and calls you on the carpet.

What's Wrong?

👄 If you were the person leaking the information, you are in deep and possibly fatal trouble.

👄 You will have minimal credibility with any of your clients after this episode.

👄 Releasing the information achieved nothing for you and your company.

👄 You may lose your job if the account goes to your competition as a result of your bad judgment.

Some Success Strategies:

Put out the fire as fast as you can! If you leaked the data, explain your reason for doing so and do it convincingly. If you didn't, issue a firm, confident denial and volunteer to help the client find out who did release the story.

#35 If It's Thursday, It Must Be Topeka

Your travel itinerary is packed so full, you hardly have time to make the dozens of sales calls you have scheduled. You bounce from one outlet to another, trying to cover as much ground as you can.

What's Wrong?

↘ You over-scheduled the number of stops you've lined up along the way.

↘ You didn't leave any time for deep discussions with any of the clients.

↘ Delegation to others is not your strong suit, leaving you the sole sales person your customers rely on.

↘ Your competition has two sales people covering the same geography as you are responsible for.

Some Success Strategies:

Organize your itinerary in such a way that you call on all your top accounts and prospects as required. Your secondary clients and prospects should receive similar attention but only after servicing your best accounts first. And, your marginal and small accounts get serviced whenever time permits. Consider having your company's telephone sales people contact the customers between your personal visits.

#36 And The Decision Is, Indecision

You deliver an exceptional presentation, but instead of getting the green light you wind up with the decision being stalled until the boss gets back from Egypt. Then she (the boss) gets sick and goes into the hospital. Still, your contact lacks authority to say "yea" or "nay."

What's Wrong?

 Now you feel sick.

 You should have known in advance that the decision would rest on the boss' shoulders.

 She should have been at the presentation.

 You wasted time, money, and effort.

 Now you have to schedule and prepare for still another trip.

Some Success Strategies:

When you review your trip checklist prior to departure, include identification of the decision-makers and double-check with them to ensure they'll be at your presentation. In certain cultures, consider taking along some small gifts to reward the bosses for being available for your presentation—and their decision.

#37 Don't Isolate Yourself From Home Or Office

You get so caught up in local activity that you forget to check in with the office or call home at the end of the day.

What's Wrong?

☎ When there's urgent information to be shared with you, no one knows where you are.

☎ You could miss valuable messages.

☎ People back home need to know where to find you, especially in emergency situations.

☎ You lose track of what's happening in your real world.

☎ Your family really misses you and needs to hear from you.

Some Success Strategies:

Install voicemail at home and in the office so you can send and receive messages any time of the day or night. Set a specific time when you will be in contact with key people and key family members. Or, use your laptop to e-mail messages via the Internet. It's quicker than a floating bottle.

#38 Fail To Be Nice To The Boss

Your boss arrives in town while you're having a leisurely spaghetti dinner and you fail to pick her up at the airport. Unfortunately, you don't have a good excuse. When you bump into her at the hotel, she seems perturbed and you don't know why.

What's Wrong?

➤ You should assume that most bosses like to be picked up by their team members.

➤ You missed the opportunity to spend quality time with someone who is difficult to corner while you're both in the home office.

➤ If you had Chinese food instead of Italian, the fortune cookie would have pre-warned you.

➤ Your oversight demonstrates that you don't respect her or her position.

Some Success Strategies:

Before your trip, find out whether your manager will be joining you at the meeting. Get her flight itinerary and ask the assistant to tell her you'll be there to meet her at the gate. Also, plan to deliver the boss back to the airport for her return flight. Be ready to update her on the issues you and the client are dealing with, and suggest how she can best support you and your organization's position.

#39 Can't Write, Listen, And Chew Gum Simultaneously

You prefer to pack light—very light. In fact, you rarely take a note pad. While everyone else is scribbling, you're listening. . . and thinking about tonight's dinner, wondering if your plane will be on time, and—suddenly, the meeting's over.

What's Wrong?

- Your laziness may lose business for your company.

- Your recall isn't the greatest.

- Because your mind is wandering, you don't contribute much to the meeting.

- The note-takers are reluctant to share their information with you.

Some Success Strategies:

If you can't discipline yourself to take good notes, get a mini cassette tape player and record your recollections immediately following the meeting. Then you'll at least have a record of what happened—but don't lose the tape. And, unless your meeting with a chewing gum manufacturer, lose the gum before you open your mouth.

#40 Paging Mr. Sherlock

You decided at the last minute to ship all of your meeting materials so as not to have to check them on the plane. Now they're lost somewhere in the hotel and you have no clues to help you find them.

What's Wrong?

○ You should know by now that you can't rely on third-party firms to track critical shipments.

○ Hotels are notorious for not keeping track of incoming shipments for guests.

○ Helping you search is annoying to the bell staff.

○ There's no time to have a duplicate shipment sent.

Some Success Strategies:

Anytime you lose control of items you absolutely must have, your colleagues begin to wonder about your ability to manage a project effectively. Despite the fact that you may have to make a few compromises, hand-carrying is the best way to ensure that you will have everything you need. If you do ship your materials, write "hold for guest arrival" on the packaging and bring the tracking numbers with you to help facilitate the delivery.

Chapter 4

It's Showtime!

#41 Drayage Is Not Something That Backs Up In Your Basement Sewer

You're not familiar with a lot of terms that are used in the trade show business. Therefore, you get stuck for a huge bill when you sign up for drayage service without checking with someone at the trade show. It turns out you didn't really need it, but only after a lot of money is paid out.

What's Wrong?

💰 At a typical trade show, the "help" comes with a large price tag.

💰 The "help" is seldom helpful, but they talk a good game.

💰 Slipping large bills under the table to the lead supervisor often nets no gains.

💰 As your money pile diminishes, so does your power over the crew.

💰 You try to do it all yourself, but suddenly your booth is being picketed.

Some Success Strategies:

There are many ways to carry out a trade show plan successfully. Naturally, experience will make the job easier as you go along. You'll learn, for example, that some crew chiefs will send four people when two will do and try to trick you into paying more than you bargained for. Some set-up crews practice ways in which they can pad their hours. Here's a hint: Be very clear about what you need and when you need it. Stand your ground and you'll won't be hassled in the future.

#42 Your Fate Is In The Hands Of The Maid

Your plan was to arrive at the hotel at 4 p.m., rest a few hours, and deliver your motivational speech at 7 p.m. You arrived at 4 p.m., but your room wasn't ready and the hotel was full. The front desk attendant refused to check you into a "dirty" room ("hotel policy, sir!"). At 5 p.m., the room still wasn't ready and you were steamed. The manager was nowhere to be found.

What's Wrong?

- There's no time left to find another hotel.

- Without some kind of rest, your speech will likely be a bomb.

- No one at the hotel appears interested in solving your problem.

- At this point, you need someone to give *you* a motivational speech.

Some Success Strategies:

Ask the front desk clerk whether you can use an open meeting or board room to rehearse your presentation. Tip him if necessary, but get him to find you any suitable room available so you can get your act together, stretch out on a couch for a few winks, and be ready when your housekeeper returns from her ski trip to Aspen and resumes her room-cleaning duties.

#43 Did You Hear The One About. . .?

In a conservative social gathering on the road, you decide to liven up the event by telling off-color jokes. Your boss overhears one of your blue stories and turns purple with anger.

What's Wrong?

- Off-color jokes should never be told during a business gathering.

- No one laughed—don't they have a sense of humor?

- The gathering dissipated after you got there, so there will be plenty of talk about your disastrous impact on the party.

- The punch line: You're in trouble.

Some Success Strategies:

Avoid being black listed. Do some fence-mending as quickly as possible. Apologize to everyone in sight, especially your boss. Send a note to the host and hostess and tell them you were on a new Slovakian drug that caused you to split your personality. Explain that it was the other you who acted so remarkably stupid. Next time, don't take chances. Save your jokes for a more appropriate occasion.

#44 Not Prepping The Boss

The boss has flown into town to support you in an important appointment with the client. However, you both got caught up in socializing last night, and he has no clue as to what to say when the client asks him specific questions.

What's Wrong?

➤ The boss is farther away from the client situation than you are.

➤ When the boss says the wrong things, it's embarrassing to you, to the boss, and to the client.

➤ Senior management isn't impressed with your lack of preparation either.

➤ It's almost impossible to cover up his ignorance of the facts.

➤ You find the whole encounter a waste of time and money.

Some Success Strategies:

It's your responsibility to ensure that he has an update before he goes into the meeting. Take the initiative to write a summary situation analysis before you leave the office and get a copy to your manager so he will be able to bone up on the essentials. Because you have provided your manager with the summary, he will be able to add value to the meeting.

#45 There's Nothing Mini About The Bill

You appreciated the convenience of reaching into the mini-bar and drinking a few bottles of beer while you were relaxing in your hotel room. When you checked out the next day, you were charged $33.00 for a 12-pack—more than double what you were used to paying in a liquor store.

What's Wrong?

 You may have to take a second mortgage on your home just to pay the mini-bar bill.

 You didn't check the costs before you opened a couple of cool ones.

 The beers gave you two headaches the next morning—and one is paying the bill.

 And you thought paying $8 on the flight for a glass of wine was bad.

Some Success Strategies:

If you feel the need to indulge in some refreshment in your room, check out the availability of a convenient store near your hotel. Pick up your supplies the first night and you'll be set for the rest of your stay. . . at normal prices. Or, if you grab one or two from the mini-bar, replace them later after you visit the local store.

#46 Some Fool Filched Your Favorite Files

You're an attorney transporting two beat-up boxes of files for an out-of-town court case. They're packed in cardboard boxes that look like they survived the battle of Bull Run. You stop to use the airport's restroom facilities and leave the files on a rusty cart outside in the aisle. When you exit the restroom, there are no files to be found in any direction.

What's Wrong?

☐ Leaving the files unattended was stupid.

☐ Without those files, your case is a goner.

☐ You have no way of duplicating the knee-deep files.

☐ Use of the computer for this kind of research is a slow, arduous process.

☐ What little faith you had in mankind has gone the way of the dodo bird.

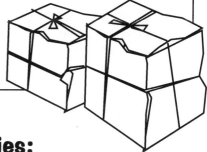

Some Success Strategies:

First, check with airport security. Maybe they called the bomb squad to have the boxes removed. No such luck? Contact your secretary and have her check your computer files to determine whether the trial files can be retrieved. When you find out they are available, contact the court and ask them to assist you in having your files sent via e-mail or as a fax. If you accomplish that step, they will repave the cyberspace lanes to ensure your material arrives as quickly as possible.

#47 Now That's Entertainment!

When it comes to entertaining your clients, you tend to chose the most lavish restaurants, order the most expensive meals, serve the best wines, and tip like there's no tomorrow.

What's Wrong?

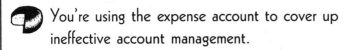 You're using the expense account to cover up ineffective account management.

You're running up substantial expense tabs and you don't have an unlimited budget.

Keep up this kind of spending and there won't be a tomorrow for you after all.

 The client is more interested in getting work done than being entertained at 3-hour lunches.

Some Success Strategies:

Be prudent in the use of your organization's resources. Coming in near or below budget is far more impressive to your boss than a large stack of receipts from expensive restaurants. Overspending is a sign of weak discipline and lack of management control of the account. If meals are on the meeting agenda, find out ahead of time where there is an appropriate, business-friendly establishment and make your reservations. Entertain as if it were your own money—unless of course you're filthy rich.

#48 Traveling Alone?

You're a single woman in a strange city for the first time. You're confident that you can handle yourself, but after your first meal in the hotel restaurant, a tough-looking guy approaches you and you have difficulty getting rid of him. From that point on, you're terrified that he might try to find you and cause big problems.

What's Wrong?

☞ You should have reported the incident immediately to the hotel manager and the security staff.

☞ You find yourself locked in your room and not wanting to come out.

☞ He's preventing you from having a good time—much less accomplishing the goals of your trip.

☞ Talking with someone like this gives you the chills. You hope he doesn't track down your phone number.

Some Success Strategies:

When something like this occurs, it's a good idea to summon the hotel manager and explain the situation. Then, ask for premium protection from the security staff. Insist that they escort you to your room. Next time wait until the restaurant is crowded. And, if you are approached, politely yet firmly end the conversation before it can begin. Pretend you don't speak his language. Try to travel with another person whenever possible. If you travel alone often, take a class in self-defense.

#49 Don't Let Your Poor Upbringing Show

You shock the other guests at an international dinner party when you eat most of the meal with your fingers and hands, and then proceed to lick your fingers, sending most of them away from the table.

What's Wrong?

☞ You flunked the basic course in table manners.

☞ Your hands are probably full of germs.

☞ You got yourself into the spotlight for all the wrong reasons.

☞ Even if you apologize now, everyone will remember your crude eating habits.

Some Success Strategies:

Get some counseling in table manners and use what you learn in your next social outing. Be sure to wash your hands before every meal and learn to use the utensils properly. When dining internationally, study the table manners of your hosts and mimic their style as best you can. Otherwise, you'll just be known as "jungle boy."

50 You're A Cool Dude

You're involved in a planning session with representatives of subsidiaries from all around the world. When you open your mouth, every foreigner's jaw drops as you regale them with American idioms and slang which leaves everyone confused.

What's Wrong?

💣 You didn't consider that they would have no clue as to what you're talking about.

💣 When you don't communicate, very little happens.

💣 You sound more like a teenager than a businesswoman.

💣 You're portraying a negative image that everyone will remember.

Some Success Strategies:

Prepare for meetings with international clients by brushing up on the basics of their languages so you can at least greet them and say a few other words they'll understand. Enroll in an international business class at a local college to learn other culture's customs. Also, since you're now an adult, learn to speak an adult language. Be aware that many slang words can be grossly misinterpreted.

#51 What's That Ship's Mast Doing Here?

You tried to save money by not visiting your meeting site beforehand. Now, you discover that the meeting room is completely inadequate for your group—especially the big post in the middle of the room.

What's Wrong?

↗ The hotel is fully booked, and you can't move your meeting to a different room.

↗ Your presentation is multimedia, and you can't just move it to one side of the room.

↗ Bawling out the sales coordinator for not telling you about the room's limitations doesn't help, either.

↗ Your going to get a shipload of heat from your manager.

Some Success Strategies:

Always find out all you can about meeting sites in advance, because you don't want, or need, any surprises at the last minute. Lack of proper preparation is a downfall of many meetings. To solve your immediate problem, meet with the sales manager and get the earliest available alternative room. Otherwise, consider moving the presentation to a different location, such as an executive suite.

#52 It's Your Secretary. Are You Here?

Your office staff is in a crisis mode while you're out of town, and everything seems to be falling apart. As a result, they are calling you every hour for advice and direction, disrupting your out-of-town meeting.

What's Wrong?

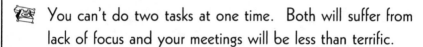 You can't do two tasks at one time. Both will suffer from lack of focus and your meetings will be less than terrific.

Your colleagues will become irritated by you constantly interrupting the meeting to answer the phone.

Solving problems hundreds of miles away is difficult at best.

You're preoccupied throughout the day and it shows.

Some Success Strategies:

Wrap up all major issues at the office before you leave on the trip. Tell your staff not to call you at the meeting location until you reach them after your meeting. Tell the client to have her secretary hold any calls that come in for you. Set your pager on "vibrate" mode and check it during breaks and lunch. In addition, direct your office staff to use voicemail and commit yourself to checking it regularly.

#53 The Little Wrinkle That Never Came Out

You wore your new $700 genuine silk suit on the plane, folded the jacket carefully, and placed it in the storage compartment above your seat. Two minutes later, along comes the local bowling ace who has his favorite silver sheen ball...and he parks his bowling ball on top of your jacket.

What's Wrong?

- When you arrive at your destination and retrieve the jacket, you complain to the flight attendant, but all you get is a shrug of the shoulders.

- There was no way to anticipate the action of the three-fingered wizard from Winnetka.

- It looks like your suit was thrown in the gutter.

- The cost of getting it cleaned and pressed is prohibitive, even if you had the time to get it done.

- You don't have a spare.

Some Success Strategies:

Don't get up from your seat in a rage and strike at the bowler, who could probably make mashed potatoes out of you. Instead, try to reason with the guy. If that fails, call the huskiest flight attendant over and explain the problem in your terms before the buzzy bowler gets in his two cents worth.

#54 Who Knows What Took Place During Your Call?

Time has a way of slipping over the horizon when you return from a trip or a series of sales meetings. You don't find it necessary to write a comprehensive trip report, because you have confidence that you will be able to remember all of the salient details.

What's Wrong?

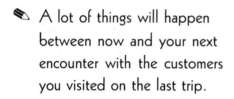

✎ A lot of things will happen between now and your next encounter with the customers you visited on the last trip.

✎ The customer doesn't remember all of the decisions that were made during your meeting.

✎ No one on your staff has any clues as to what transpired during your client visits.

✎ You face embarrassment if you can't recall significant issues that were raised during your discussion.

Some Success Strategies:

While you are en route back to your home base, write or dictate a complete listing of the issues and decisions that were achieved during your calls. Have it typed up and distributed to the appropriate staff members and to the client. If there were any misinterpretations, let them surface right now, before more time flies by.

#55 How To Lose Control Of Your Destiny

Racing to the airport for your return flight always takes more time than you anticipate. This time you're real short on time, so you drop off the car and run to the airline check-in counter without picking up your rental car bill. That sets up an unpleasant surprise when you get the invoice in the mail.

What's Wrong?

◆ Since you weren't present to defend yourself, they charged you for body damage and fuel.

◆ Contesting unfair charges through the mail is practically useless.

◆ You have no way to prove the car was free of body damage when you turned it in.

◆ There are no loopholes to drive through.

Some Success Strategies:

Allow plenty of time to get to the airport. Allow time for a few wrong turns, to fill up the fuel tank, stand in line to check in your car, and get a receipt to attach to your expense report. When you rush in and drop off the car without resolving your bill, you'll be at the mercy of the rental car company, and they will always protect their interests first. As for this one, you're stuck, my friend.

Chapter 5

Health Is Wealth

#56 Watch Your Back

Your suitcase is huge. In fact, it's big enough to hold your entire wardrobe along with a small selection of books and videos. And, just for good measure, you throw in your boom box.

What's Wrong

Lifting your suitcase will be a struggle.

The airlines will charge you extra for the additional weight.

The bellman at the hotel will demand a bigger tip.

You'll injure your back at the worst possible time and you won't have any medication with you.

Your chiropractor is not with you either.

Some Success Strategies:

Don't bring anything that you won't be needing including keys, clothes you'll never wear, your bowling ball, etc. For a small fee, some hotels now offer computers, fax machines, and printers in the guest rooms which means you can leave yours at home. Consider shipping your business materials ahead of time via express courier and bring return labels with you to ship them back. When packing, pack on top of a dresser or other high surface rather than the bed. Constant bending is a constant risk and when you finally do bend over to pick up your case, your ability to return to the full upright and locked position is greatly reduced.

#57 For Here, Or To Go?

You live on fast food while you're on the road. It's cheap, quick, convenient, and you don't have to dress up to eat. You're proud to show your boss how much you save in meal expenses on every trip.

What's Wrong?

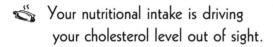 Your nutritional intake is driving your cholesterol level out of sight.

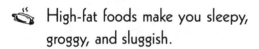 High-fat foods make you sleepy, groggy, and sluggish.

You never met a calorie you didn't salivate over.

The money you save goes to the doctor when you get back.

It's embarrassing when your customer finds your briefcase full of kid's meal toys, and you don't have children.

Some Success Strategies:

Good nutrition is a basic ingredient for keeping fit on the road. Check caloric and fat content prior to ordering your meals, and make sure you maintain a balanced diet. Bring along your vitamins to help supplement your diet on the road. In some foreign countries, you have to drink bottled water or you'll be the opposite of sluggish.

#58 Feeling Ill?
You Probably Are

You're feeling under the weather. You think by "toughing it out," you'll prove to your client that you're a real go-getter and not even a slight case of the flu can stop you from making that presentation.

What's Wrong?

☼ If you spread the illness to others, they'll remember you for not having the common sense to stay home.

☼ Your company image may suffer by your substandard performance.

☼ You may say something while heavily medicated that will prove you're really ill.

☼ Your physical condition will deteriorate as you attempt to work despite your illness.

Some Success Strategies:

Call your boss early and explain the problem. Suggest a substitute or cancel the presentation until you're feeling better. Have him call the client and explain the dilemma you're facing. Chances are they'll be glad to reschedule. If you're already in the client city, ask them to refer you to a good local doctor. In addition, it's a good idea to carry basic medications with you to ward off any possible headaches, sinus conditions, upset stomachs, etc.

#59 The Pain Is
Mainly On The Plain

You're in Spain, munching roasted El Toro with salsa, when your biggest filling comes loose from your tooth and falls out. Now the nerve is exposed and it's very painful.

What's Wrong?

 You don't know the first thing about Spanish dentistry or dentists.

 It hurts so much, you can hardly talk (in English or Spanish).

 You can't make it through the rest of your trip with an open cavity.

 You don't have any adhesive that would work.

 Getting to the root of the problem will be difficult.

Some Success Strategies:

Talk to your local hosts or the concierge at your hotel to get a referral to a dentist you can trust. Have your hosts call for an appointment and explain your predicament. Also, have them get a cost estimate before any work is done. As with most dental problems, prevention is the key. As such, see your local family dentist regularly so that you can nip these potential disasters in the bud.

#60 Don't Give Up Your Tone While Out-Of-Town

You forgot to bring your exercise gear on the trip and lose the opportunity to keep yourself in tip-top shape. As a result, you feel out of sorts and out of synch all week.

What's Wrong?

- You don't think you'll have time to work out, but you do.

- You don't think the hotel will have work-out facilities, but they do.

- You thought you'd be the only one exercising, but you're not.

- You feel you can skip a week without exercise, and nothing will change, but it does.

Some Success Strategies:

Make your exercise gear one of the "musts" to take along when you travel. Most hotels have fitness centers available for their guests. Some may charge a small fee so make sure you check the price before you take part. Even a walk is better than nothing when more rigorous exercise is restricted by time or facilities. Always keep good habits going without interruption.

#61 Special Meals Help Your Disposition And Waistline

You've often wondered why the flight attendants call out names at meal time and deliver food to those who respond, before anyone else is served. Then you find out you should have found out earlier what you just found out.

What's Wrong?

- You worry about the nutritional value in airline meals but don't realize you have options.

- You hate to stick out in a crowd. You'd rather be like the other sheep and gobble down the standard fare.

- You heard about special meals years ago, but you thought they were only for sick people.

- You actually may like airline food.

Some Success Strategies:

Be vigilant. Airline and airport foods are generally high in fat and low in nutrition. Your best bet? Order a vegetarian meal when you book your flight, pack a meal, or wait until you land, if your stomach permits. Proper nutrition on the road will help you overcome jet lag and help prevent illness. Also, be prepared for the shorter flights that don't provide any meal service. Oftentimes, you will end up taking two or three of these flights back to back just to get where you're going. This could mean six to eight hours without food.

Chapter 6

Now You Become
The Foreigner

#62 Is Overseas Travel Different Than Domestic? Si And Oui

You show up at the airport without a current passport and the necessary visas for your trip overseas. Then you act surprised when you get turned away and left behind.

What's Wrong?

🖑 You'll be inconvenienced, stymied, and embarrassed at every turn.

🖑 You won't be able to accomplish your goals.

🖑 You may not even get there.

🖑 You think cultural diversity is something grown in a petri dish.

Some Success Strategies:

If you're traveling overseas for the first time, find out as much as you can about foreign travel. Be aware of both the significant and small differences and avoid being humiliated by preparing well in advance. Talk to others who have been where you're going, read about your destinations, and discuss your questions with your travel agent. As you gain knowledge, you'll also gain confidence.

#63 You Encounter A Major Distraction: Homesickness

You planned your overseas trip carefully, and everything is in order. But on this first journey across the ocean, you encounter an obstacle to success that you hadn't planned on: You're homesick, and you really miss your family.

What's Wrong?

🏠 You haven't experienced this problem before, but you've also never been this far from home before.

🏠 It's very expensive to call home, although your spouse's familiar voice would do wonders for your morale.

🏠 You can't concentrate on anything, because you're constantly thinking of your wife, the kids, the dog, the parakeet, and how long your grass is getting.

🏠 Your loneliness is affecting your ability to do business.

Some Success Strategies:

This problem will be less of a distraction on future trips, but you can maintain connections with your family by faxing a message and requesting an early reply, by using e-mail, or by calling home during late night hours to minimize costs. Another solution is to bring along personal memorabilia like family photos, and tapes of local radio programs to remind you of your other world. Consider bringing the family along with you for an overseas vacation. Keep in touch with current events by watching CNN.

#64 Who Ordered The Interpreter?

Your meeting in a foreign land didn't get off to the greatest start. Neither you nor your customer speak the other person's language. A call has gone out for an interpreter but, in the meantime, you're doodling and looking at the sights of Tokyo outside the window.

What's Wrong?

✋ If you had done your homework, you would have discovered that no one had requested an interpreter.

✋ Now you're going to have to pay premium rates.

✋ You didn't check to find out whether the client speaks English. And, to be fair, he didn't check with you either.

✋ Sign language doesn't work when you're focusing on complicated negotiations.

✋ The client is upset and may not be in a positive mood when you begin negotiations.

Some Success Strategies:

Whenever you travel to a foreign country, you must keep the language distinction as a top-of-mind look-out. Even if your contact speaks fluent English, there is a lot of room for misinterpretation. Get a good interpreter and save yourself a Yankee-sized load of problems. Avoid using Americanized slang and jargon.

#65 And Now, Señor, We Interrupt Your Siesta

You're in Spain to interview prospective advertising agencies and your host takes you to lunch which begins with drinks, a couple of toasts, some salad, an entree with wine sauce, and after-dinner drinks.
Then they park you in a dark room and present their reel of radio spots
. . . in Spanish.

What's Wrong?

- You had too much to drink and pass out after the first 30 second tape.

- You can't apologize for your rudeness . . . they don't understand much English anyway.

- You can't wait to get back to your hotel room so you can take a long nap.

- There's no way you'll accomplish your objectives for this trip at this rate.

Some Success Strategies:

When you select the candidates, it's a good idea to let them know that you don't speak their language so they can arrange for interpreters. When you dine on trips like this one, control your consumption of alcohol—even at the risk of offending your host, who would prefer to negotiate with you when you're smashed. Don't sign anything without a clear head.

#66 Oops!

You forget about the time difference and rouse your boss from a deep sleep at 3:30 a.m. Unfortunately, you also have nothing important to report to him. He is not easily amused under normal circumstances, but, as the minutes pass, he gets downright livid.

What's Wrong?

☎ You interrupted one of his more pleasant dreams.

☎ In the morning, he's going to tell everyone at the office that you're a dumb, inconsiderate bleep.

☎ He doesn't believe your comment that you worked hard that day and made considerable progress.

☎ He's already plotting revenge.

☎ Now you're wondering what kind of reception you're going to receive when you get back to the office.

Some Success Strategies:

Remind the boss that he was once a neophyte and probably made some dumb mistakes of his own. If he tells you that he never made similar bonehead moves, fall off your chair onto the floor, laughing and holding your sides. Maybe he'll capture the spirit of the situation and forgive you. Next time, leave him a voice mail instead.

#67 Rome Isn't Exactly Like Omaha

You volunteer to drive a rental car in Rome, even though you've never driven a car in Europe. In fact, you've never been in Rome. So here you are, surrounded by taxis, motor scooters, bicycles, buggies, cars, trucks, broken-down wagons, and pedestrians trying to cross the street in traffic.

What's Wrong?

- You didn't start off in the best of circumstances. You're stuck in traffic with no place to go.

- And, wouldn't you know? You're in an urgent rush to meet the distributor.

- The controls on the car are very different from what you normally drive.

- You don't understand street and directional signs.

- And, you're on the wrong side of the road.

Some Success Strategies:

Take some time on the road to acclimate yourself to the whims and foibles of European drivers. And do it away from the city, where you'll have some margin for error. Driving in the city is challenging enough in your home country, let alone on foreign soil. If you're in Asia, don't even think about it—take a taxi.

#68 Those Windmills Were, Ah, Great?

Your camera batteries are run down, the film is for indoor use only, and you brought the wrong lens. Otherwise, everything is perfect.

What's Wrong?

📷 You fail to appreciate the significance of famous landmarks.

📷 Photography is not your favorite hobby.

📷 You always deal in the present, and don't consider the potential value of pictures when you look back in a few years.

📷 You think it's a hassle to get equipment and film together.

📷 You're not very focused on your trip.

Some Success Strategies:

You can develop a long-lasting rapport with your overseas hosts by taking pictures of them and sending prints with brief notes. Plus, you'll have interesting photos to help recall the good things about travel when you're older. Your kids and grand kids will enjoy them again and again. If taking photos during your trips is not possible, buy some local post cards instead.

#69 Why The Fuss? It's Only Paris!

You jet into town, race in a taxi to the trade show, bury yourself in the hotel, and race to the airport. Isn't travel wonderful?

What's Wrong?

✧ Your vision is narrow and your time limited.

✧ In the end, you feel unfulfilled, as if you mechanically went through the motions.

✧ You weren't excited about going, and you're even less excited to ever go back.

✧ Life in the fast lane will surely make you lose your mind.

✧ You're missing out.

Some Success Strategies:

After you get back home, you'll regret you didn't take more time to see and experience the highlights of countries you visited. Allow enough time to visit landmarks, dine in foreign restaurants, and experience different cultures. Next time, ask the local hosts to set you up for a tour and the chance to meet a native family.

#70 What Are These Ladies Doing In The Men's Room?

You didn't bother to learn any of the basic language and symbols for facilities in foreign countries and now you're standing in the middle of the ladies' rest room, blushing while they're flushing. You're about to learn one new word, however: gendarme.

What's Wrong?

✐ You're embarrassed and your restroommates are angry.

✐ You need directions to the men's room, but everyone speaks French.

✐ The police have been called to haul you away. There may be a men's room in the police station. That's "maybe."

✐ You quickly discovered that this is not a good place to pick up dates.

Some Success Strategies:

Get a language tape and guidebook and study it intensely so you can navigate without getting in trouble. Learn a few basic phrases so you can communicate on simple matters. Right now, the police are gesturing as if they're going to hurl you into the Seine for doing such a dastardly deed.

#71 Passport Is Nowhere To Be Found

You used your passport yesterday and now you've lost it. You look everywhere, but it still doesn't turn up. You feel like a man without a country.

What's Wrong?

☹ You're not familiar with the process to obtain a new passport.

☹ The nearest consulate is hundreds of miles away.

☹ You're concerned that someone could be posing as you.

☹ You're afraid you won't be able to return to your home country.

Some Success Strategies:

Track down the U.S. Embassy or nearest U.S. government agency. They'll have detailed instructions on how to get a temporary passport or visa to tide you over until you get home. Always carry a photo copy of your passport in a separate location. This will facilitate a speedy replacement. In the future, try not to be such a Stupid Business Traveler. Keep your passport in the same spot between trips.

#72 Do They All Have To Cry At Once?

You bring a big luggage bag full of presents for your client's children and every one of them burns out because of the voltage differential. The kids are very disappointed and your generosity is somewhat overlooked.

What's Wrong?

- You didn't expect to have a problem. Now you have to haul the toys back to the U.S., have them repaired if possible, and ship them back.

- You'll have to pay duties and taxes on them for the second time.

- The gifts might get damaged again during shipping.

- Once the kids see the toys for a second time, all the elements of surprise and excitement will be gone.

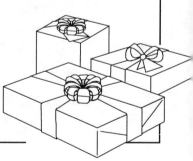

Some Success Strategies:

Under the circumstances, you'd be better off buying gifts locally. The kids would be mollified. There wouldn't be any conversion problem. And you get off the hook. You might ask your client ahead of time what his children would enjoy from your home country.

#73 Y'all Pass The Figs, Mohammed!

You didn't research your destination in advance, and now you're the only one in the room wearing a tie, suit coat, and shoes. The host asks you to propose a toast and you announce that you prefer whole wheat. And when the sales manager passes the bottle of Aquavit when you're peeling shrimp, you gulp down a half of a bottle before coming up for air.

What's Wrong?

- You made a fool of yourself without even knowing it.

- You're troubled by the volume of giggling you're hearing.

- If you drink too much of the Aquavit without even knowing what it is, you'll be sorry in the morning.

- Your hangover the next morning makes you feel that your head is inside a giant bell.

- You're about to be dinged by a donger.

Some Success Strategies:

Knowing local customs—especially those that surface in business meals—is a tremendous asset when you're trying to make a positive impression for yourself and your corporation. If you don't drink alcoholic beverages, politely thank your host for the generous offer and decline.

#74 Wasting Money Is An Expensive Habit

You commit all of the typical rookie errors—paying gratuities on meals when they're already included, failing to document purchases so you can get a tax refund, and misunderstanding the value of local currency.

What's Wrong?

$ You didn't talk to veteran travelers while planning your trip.

$ Currency is flowing through your pockets faster than you can count it.

$ Good records and receipt copies are needed to claim tax refunds.

$ You probably saved very little on purchases.

$ You don't know how or where to apply for rebates.

Some Success Strategies:

Discuss this subject with your travel agent before you leave, and get plenty of advice on ways to conserve funds. And don't lose track of receipts. Expect that gratuities are already covered in meal costs. If you're not sure, ask before you pay. Read a book on rules of foreign etiquette.

#75 Ugly Americans Should Stay Home

When you visit foreign countries, you're always tired, short-tempered, and often yell to get someone to understand you. For some reason, that doesn't result in better service.

What's Wrong?

❁ You intimidate service people and you're not well-liked, to say the least.

❁ As a representative of your country, you're creating negative stereotypes.

❁ You also don't tip well, and word gets around fast.

❁ Your bombastic behavior is childish and attracts a lot of attention.

❁ Most people try to avoid you and don't want to have anything to do with you.

Some Success Strategies:

Talk to other people you travel with and ask them to level with you. Based on their input, make a serious effort to demonstrate more class and finesse and see what that gets you on your next trip. Always be courteous. Leave the desk-pounding and profane language to some other jerk.

#76 Don't Leave This Kind Of Paper Trail

After a round of meetings at fancy hotels in Europe, you leave several hotels without settling your accounts. You figure you'll never be back there again, and they won't track you down to get their bills paid once you're safely back within the U.S. borders.

What's Wrong?

- You're talking basic dishonesty here. Think again!

- You're making assumptions that may not be accurate.

- You're leaving a trail of negative images for your company.

- You should have budgeted for these expenses so they could be paid on a timely basis.

- When your controller finds out about this, she'll have a financial fit.

Some Success Strategies:

It's always a good idea to pay bills on time. If you have disputes, express them in writing and hold up payment of those specific items until they're resolved. But pay the rest of the bill when you check out, to keep your credit rating solid. Never underestimate the ability of a foreign bill collector.

Chapter 7

Absolute No-No's
While Traveling

#77 Pass The Contract With The Ketchup, Please

You're invited to the client's home for a social evening with his family. Suddenly, the conversation turns to business, and the whole family is listening to the two of you discuss key negotiating points. And then they join in.

What's Wrong?

- You're put at a tremendous disadvantage and he has all of the leverage, not to mention the home court advantage.

- He's taking advantage of your "nice guy" disposition.

- You're unprepared to do business.

- Your files are back at the hotel.

Some Success Strategies:

Get a clear understanding before you go to his home as to whether any business will be conducted during the evening. Then, advise your host that you would like to conclude the business discussion before you meet the rest of the family. Never try to mix the two.

#78 Picking The Cheapest Hotel

Choosing the most inexpensive place to stay doesn't always make sense. For example, your choice this time positions you in the worst part of town, and when you go out to start your car there's nothing to start. Car's gone. At least you saved $40 on the hotel room.

What's Wrong?

☆ You should have checked out the location more carefully.

☆ Your personal safety is at stake.

☆ You've got to rent another car.

☆ You should really check out and move, but you hate to pay more money.

☆ It doesn't matter anyway, since you left your wallet in the car.

Some Success Strategies:

The world of travel, like the global environment in which we live, is changing a little bit each day. Therefore, it is very important that you keep abreast of these changes, be aware of the security issues that concern hotel management, and anticipate a problem rather than reacting to it. Stay at a hotel where you're well-protected, even if it costs more. And always be aware of the potential dangers that exist in today's cities and suburbs.

#79 The Uninvited Guest

You show up at the client site with a colleague you introduce as someone who is in training with you. Your guest listens intently to everything that is discussed during the meeting and keeps copies of handouts. The client obviously becomes edgy and uncomfortable.

What's Wrong?

💣 You didn't clear the presence of the guest before you arrived for the meeting.

💣 The customer has suspicions about the person tagging along with you.

💣 Your "guest" starts to ask basic questions—all of which are basically stupid.

💣 Your guest is not adding value to this meeting.

Some Success Strategies:

You should have had the sense to clear this intrusion with the customer long before the meeting. Now it's a real irritant to your customer, and it's standing in the way of a successful conclusion to your trip. Level with the customer by apologizing for not seeking prior approval. If you're training this person, be sure to fully prepare them for each and every meeting beforehand.

#80 Kids. . . Guess What?

You pack up the family and head out of town, hoping to spend quality time with them while you handle your business chores. In the morning, your son splits his lip on the night stand and you have to get him stitched up in the local hospital.

What's Wrong?

- You're late for an important meeting.

- Kids and business preparations don't mix well.

- One or the other will get less attention than they deserve.

- Your client is less than sympathetic.

- With all these distractions, you have difficulty keeping on schedule.

Some Success Strategies:

While the intent may be noble, don't try mixing business with family affairs. Enjoy family time when it's not overshadowed by business pressures. Some kids think it's cute to cut up Daddy's favorite tie. If you do feel compelled to combine a business trip with a family trip, consider adding days onto the front end or back end of your trip rather than overlapping the two.

#81 A Fool And His Luggage Are Soon Parted

Upon arrival to your hotel, the bellman graciously grabs your baggage and whisks it into the hotel lobby while you check in. Unfortunately, while your back is turned and the bellman returns to the entrance, your unwatched luggage is whisked away by professional thieves who specialize in ripping off rookies.

What's Wrong?

 You took your eyes off your valuables.

 Not all hotels have a security battalion to watch over you and the other 2,000 guests.

 Your passport, computer, tickets, briefcase, and golf clubs will soon belong to the highest bidder—at a street auction.

 It's not likely that the crooks will return your presentation materials either.

Some Success Strategies:

Keep an eye on your luggage. Scam artists target airports and hotels. Purchase good locks for all of your luggage and business items. Tag you luggage inside and out for easy identification should it turn up. If your belongings do get hijacked, report the theft immediately to the hotel and local authorities. Ask the bellman for your tip back, you're going to need it.

#82 It Was Right There On The Desk!

You brought your laptop computer along to make your presentation. After breakfast in the dining room and some shopping in the hotel gift store, you returned to your room to find the laptop gone.

What's Wrong?

🖫 You didn't take special measures to prevent the theft.

🖫 You neglected to read the posting at the front desk that says, "Hotel Not Responsible for . . ."

🖫 Your entire presentation is on the hard drive and you don't have a backup disk.

🖫 You should have insured your computer.

🖫 Reporting the crime will eat up gigabytes of your time.

Some Success Strategies:

Take along a computer lock to affix your computer to a heavy dresser leg or to the air conditioner in your room. Make it difficult for the crook to get it out of your room; at the very least, delay the robber enough to get the police on his or her trail. Don't leave valuables in plain view. Have your travel coordinator book you into hotel rooms that have safes to lock up valuable equipment.

#83 Cost Is More Than A Four-Letter Word

You take an expense advance for your trip and find you're out of cash halfway through the itinerary. Looking back on what happened, you realize that you spent $3.15 for a can of soda, $10.95 for a hamburger, $17.00 for parking overnight, and $12.00 to send a five-page fax back to your office.

What's Wrong?

💰 You find out very quickly that your costs are running higher than you anticipate.

💰 Your cash reserve is going to be nonexistent in a matter of days.

💰 Your colleagues are booked at the same hotel and they don't seem to have a problem with the cost levels.

💰 You haven't looked for inexpensive restaurants and alternative parking lots to cut costs.

Some Success Strategies:

When you check into a hotel, be sure to gain early control of your food, beverage, supplies, and entertainment costs in the general area where you will be staying. If there are restaurants available outside of the hotel, you'll likely find the prices are lower. The same holds true for supplies. But to find out what outside sources charge, don't call these establishments from your room. The cost there is at least $1.25 per local call. Using the lobby phone will enable you to reach your party without emptying your bank accounts.

#84 Collecting The Wrong Kind Of Souvenirs

You have a habit of picking up matchbooks from hotels, restaurants, and other sites visited. You proceed to throw them in your luggage to be carried home. When you arrive home, you notice a burn hole in your favorite bag—next to your new bag of matchbooks.

What's Wrong?

🔥 You didn't realize that matches could set fire to your baggage.

🔥 Everyone on the flight is placed in jeopardy.

🔥 Thinking first is not one of your strong suits.

🔥 In addition, your favorite bag is ruined.

🔥 More often than not, you throw away the matchbooks when you return home anyway.

Some Success Strategies:

Be sensible in acquiring souvenirs and make sure you will value the items when you get them home. Select items that reflect the uniqueness of the location you visited. Never carry anything flammable in your luggage or on your person when you are flying. If you smoke, quit!

#85 That Looks Amazingly Like A Gun, Sir!

You decide to carry a weapon to protect yourself. But the metal detector is triggered at the first check point. Before you know it, you're in jail charged with a felony.

What's Wrong?

✸ This was a dumb idea from the start.

✸ The presence of a gun compromises everyone's safety.

✸ You ignored the fact that airlines prosecute anyone with a weapon.

✸ You have no bail money.

✸ The jailer keeps staring at you as if you're a mass murderer.

Some Success Strategies:

Call your attorney and describe point blank what happened. Ask him or her to post bail. Then get to work on your defense, citing stupidity as your prime motivator. If you fear your destination so much that you feel you need protection, don't go. Besides, guns are made to kill. Nothing more, nothing less. Ask yourself, "Do I want to kill?" If you answered "yes," visit the nearest mental institution as soon as possible, and leave your weapons at home.

#86 Yes, I'll Have The Goat Head Soup, Please

You're in a foreign land that speaks a foreign language and writes in foreign words. You stop at a local restaurant to indulge yourself in the local foreign fare. This foreign land also has a foreign menu. You're hungry so you decide to live dangerously and point to something that you think looks good.

What's Wrong

- After you point out what you want on the menu, your waiter begins to laugh uncontrollably.

- You may get sick from eating something that your digestive system is unaccustomed to.

- You're still obligated to pay the check whether you eat the goat's head or not.

- You're still hungry.

- Foreign culture may dictate that you eat what you get anyway or you'll upset the maitre de.

Some Success Strategies:

When traveling to a foreign country that speaks and writes in a language you don't understand, bring along a handy pocket-reference guide. These little books can act as your translator while on the road. Some languages are available in electronic versions that fit in the palm of your hand. Another good idea is to travel with someone who speaks the language. It can be a great experience to venture out to get a taste of the local culture. Just make sure that whatever you taste doesn't end up biting you back.

#87 You Figure The Travel Agent Will Cost More

You want to book as many arrangements through an authorized travel agent as you can. But, you have a feeling they charge for their services, and you don't want your travel budget to escalate.

What's Wrong?

- ✈ You haven't taken the time to find a professional agent.

- ✈ In addition, you haven't met a travel agent you feel would do a good job.

- ✈ Your thinking is outmoded, outdated, and you've been outsmarted.

- ✈ You're afraid a travel agent will sell you more travel services than you need.

Travel Agent

Some Success Strategies:

Like most areas of business today, travel is getting more and more complex. There are more choices, more packages, and more conditions than ever before. Keeping up with all this information will drive you crazy. A professional travel agent would probably cut your costs significantly and give you many more options than you will get by calling airlines directly. Using an agent will save you time, money, and headaches!

#88 My Plan For Tomorrow?

You plan to see both the primary customer and her main competitor back-to-back. You say to yourself, "What harm can this cause?" Without a second thought, you book your airline reservations.

What's Wrong?

☞ Some customers will be totally outraged by your action.

☞ Others will take it in stride and immediately call your competition.

☞ You think you can keep your contacts a secret, but you haven't heard the grapevine lately.

☞ When you tell them that your predecessor at the company did the same thing for years, they threaten to sue your firm.

☞ They wonder how many of their engineering secrets have been carried through the lobby on their way to the competitor.

Some Success Strategies:

To regain their confidence, ask them to work with you to design the kind of three-way relationship that will work for them as well as for you. Tell them you can't afford to be without either account and work out a solution with their input leading the way. Then, take every possible precaution to ensure that competitive information will never leak out.

#89 What's That Ticking In Your Suitcase, Monsieur?

You probably would have gotten away with a batch of souvenirs from your hotel room if you hadn't taken the clock. The ticking sound roused the security guards from their customary slumber.

What's Wrong?

- You should have bought a clock at the gift shop.

- You never really do anything with the things you take from hotels.

- You overheard the manager who caught you say something about a maximum security prison on the west side of the state.

- You sent the metal detector crew into an uproar.

Some Success Strategies:

Keep your luggage reserved for clothes. Don't stroll around airports with metal sculptures and mementos banging around in your bag. Be honest and leave the hotel's property in the hotel.

#90 Discuss Pricing? Are You Crazy?

The sales manager of your competitor is a friendly woman and you decide to have coffee with her during a trade association function. During the course of your informal discussion, she asks you what you're charging for a XXX Widget, a device both of your companies sell.

What's Wrong?

↪ If discovered, this conversation could get you into a heap of legal trouble.

↪ Price fixing is a serious offense.

↪ It's not a good idea to mix with the competition under any circumstances.

↪ Her request for a copy of your price sheet should be ignored.

Some Success Strategies:

Whenever you're at an industry event, there's always the possibility that you'll be asked about your pricing policies, incentive programs, or other details that should be considered proprietary information. Whenever the competition is around, there's a good rule of thumb: Don't tell them anything!

#91 Oh, Fred, There's Just One More Thing

You're winding up some discussions and your customer asks you for a job—at your company! You're taken by surprise and stumble through your response. She indicates that she would relocate to your city if she were given the job.

What's Wrong?

○ You're smack in the middle of discussing a very sensitive topic.

○ You can't believe the client's frankness in pursuing this subject with you.

○ You want to show her you're listening to her "pitch," but you know right away that she would be a poor addition to your staff.

○ This is a very awkward predicament, but you must work your way out of the encounter with finesse.

Some Success Strategies:

Explain that you didn't expect this show of interest and you will have to have time to consider it and talk with your boss about her candidacy. Ask her if her company is aware of her desire to leave, and point out that it will be necessary for your company to get permission from the client before they could hire her—if something is available.

#92 Batteries Not Included

After an extremely hectic trip away from home and family, you arrive at the airport and dash into the airport gift shop to buy some cheap trinkets for your kids. After all, you're feeling guilty about being away from them all week and you feel obligated to buy them something to prove to them you've been thinking about them day and night.

What's Wrong?

🚀 Within five minutes you've acquired a bag of junk at prices so high, they have their own flight numbers.

🚀 You're unable to put any thought into an appropriate gift.

🚀 The extra baggage is a hassle to carry and you've already checked your luggage.

🚀 You think T-shirts with the name of a city on it is a fashion statement.

Some Success Strategies:

Gifts are always a good idea when acquired for the right reasons. Your kids miss you just as much as you miss them. A gift won't replace the lost time. However, an appropriate gift can be an excellent conduit for sharing your journey with others. For example, bringing back something that is unique to the city or country you visited will help educate your family and friends about other places and cultures. Ask some of the locals for suggestions and buy them when you're not in a hurry. If you're the gift buying type, set aside time to do so. Pack them carefully so they don't get broken and don't forget your associates at work who helped make your business trip a success.

#93 Trying To Take Currency Out Of The Country

You attempt to smuggle a large volume of cash out of the country hoping to make a killing by exchanging it at a sizable profit. But your plot backfires, and now you're in trouble.

What's Wrong?

- You chose to ignore the posted limit that can be taken out by one individual.

- You were greedy and tried to take advantage of the system.

- Now you may have to pay a huge fine.

- Jail is also a possibility.

- Ignorance of the law is no excuse.

Some Success Strategies:

Learn what your limitations are in international commerce and abide by the laws of the country you are in. Sometimes penalties for transgressions of the law are much tougher than in your own country, so don't try to live outside of the law.

Chapter 8

Post-Trip Recovery, Regrouping, Recreation

#94 Don't Be A Groggy Hero

Knowing that your desk is piled up with mail and return phone call messages, you're tempted to go right back to the office upon your return from an overseas trip. Even though you feel less than terrific, you're convinced that it's important to get caught up as soon as possible.

What's Wrong?

☞ Your body hasn't had the time to readjust to the time difference and rid itself of jet lag.

☞ Your mind needs rest between the hectic days of your trip and the even busier days ahead.

☞ Without rest, you'll be working less efficiently.

☞ You fail to realize that your family needs to spend time with you and catch up on the highlights of your trip.

Some Success Strategies:

As you prepare for an overseas trip, plan at least one day as a buffer between your arrival back home and your return to work. You'll find that you'll tire quickly each day following your return, and you won't want to run your system down to empty by overstressing it just to catch up a day early. Take some time to readjust gradually. Handle business priorities by phone whenever possible.

#95 Take The Family To Dinner? No Time Tonight, Dear

As soon as you return home from a business trip, you've been on the phone and buried in your briefcase. Your family is anxious to spend quality time with you, without the distractions of your job activities.

What's Wrong?

🦊 You have your priorities mixed up.

🦊 You are nervous and anxious about some of the issues raised during the trip.

🦊 You feel you can always catch up with your lost family time.

🦊 Your family feels neglected.

Some Success Strategies:

Over the long run, you'll come to realize that nothing is more important in your life than your family. Not money. Not a fancy car. Not a high-level job. If you put your family first, you'll live a balanced life and your professional development will not be encumbered by family problems. Take your family out to dinner—even if you are tired of eating in restaurants.

#96 Where Is The Shoe Box?

Tracking expenses while on the road has never been one of your strong suits. Furthermore, you let weeks go by before you complete your expense reports. Now you can't find the receipts and your memory fails you.

What's Wrong?

☞ You neglected to get your report together on a timely basis and now you're scrambling.

☞ If your documentation is poor, you can't prove you spent any of your cash.

☞ You are unaware of the government tax documentation requirements for expenses above a certain amount and that your company may have similar requirements.

☞ Any reimbursement check owed to you will be delayed in processing.

Some Success Strategies:

The secret to successful expense management is to devise a sound system for tracking and reporting expenses and stick to it. The first thing to do is to maintain a daily record of expenditures. Second, fill out your expense report as you go along. Third, submit it right after the trip is concluded. Fourth, operate on the company's money, not your own. Fifth, don't mix personal and business expenses.

#97 Can-See-The-Air Level?

When asked by the registration clerk at the hotel if you would like to upgrade to the Concierge level for an extra $30.00, you thought he was asking if you were interested in the smog report. You declined by saying, "That's okay, I'm only here for a few days. I don't think the smog will bother me that much."

What's Wrong

👓 You miss out on the advantages of being on the Concierge floor such as a morning meal and evening hors d'oeuvres.

👓 After spending thousands on transportation, business entertainment, etc., the extra cost to be on the Concierge level is negligible.

👓 Without these services, you'll end up wasting time in the hotel's crowded restaurants, coffee shops, and checkout lines.

👓 Your competitors are charting a new strategy over a carefree breakfast on the Concierge level.

Some Success Strategies:

If the hotel has a Concierge level, consider booking your room there. The additional cost for the room is not that much more and when you factor in the free food, beverages, and services, you're nearly at break even. You'll save time as well from the benefit of express check-in and check-out along with additional staff to serve your needs. Besides, you're the one on the road, you deserve a little pampering.

#98 Revisit Trip Problems Instantly

Now that you're back home, you're anxious to get caught up with your home and social life and the backup of work waiting for you in the office. But you're still steaming about overcharges and other problems you had at the hotel where you stayed during the convention.

What's Wrong?

🏠 You don't realize you're exhausted from the rigors of the trip.

🏠 The more time that goes by, the more difficult it will be to resolve the problems.

🏠 Since you were traveling solo, no one else can take care of the matter for you.

🏠 You'd like to move on, but you hate to have $200 go down the drain.

Some Success Strategies:

Be meticulous in your scrutiny of bills while you're on trips. It's much easier to get things solved on the spot than following up via correspondence. One major obstacle is the language barrier; currency is another complication, and you'll probably also encounter arrogance from hotel management. Don't let them get away with over charging you.

#99 No Gifts?
Oh, What A Scrooge!

While you were traveling overseas, you bought gifts for your clients and your family members, but forgot the people who worked so hard to make your travel successful—your colleagues and co-workers. You've noticed a cold atmosphere around the office since you returned, and you don't know why.

What's Wrong?

☺ They all expect some small tokens of appreciation for their extra effort, and you let them down.

☺ If you don't rectify the situation, it may result in substandard work.

☺ Your colleagues think you're an ungrateful cheapskate.

☺ They'll think twice about getting you a birthday present.

☺ You dove right into the stack of work that had piled up without thinking about rewarding the department.

Some Success Strategies:

Rectify the situation quickly and decisively. Take them all out to a nice restaurant for lunch and pick up the tab. Admit to them that you screwed up and ask them to give you a second chance to come through. And next time, purchase an appropriate gift to express your appreciation for their efforts.

#100 Begin Planning For The Next Trip

You get yourself immersed in the day-to-day activity right away, and don't pause to reflect on ways your previous trip could have been more productive.

What's Wrong?

☞ You're not taking the time to rehash the pluses and minuses of the trip.

☞ You could be headed down a path where your past mistakes are repeated over and over again.

☞ There aren't any files to reference for the next time you leave on a long trip.

☞ Any information you bring back will be useless if you don't take the time to pull it all together.

☞ Your travel agent will also repeat the same mistakes while working with you and everyone else.

Some Success Strategies:

Shut off your catch-up routine for a half of one day. Take notes throughout your trip of the things you forgot to bring. Meet with your staff and the travel agent to review details of the trip, so they know what happened and why. The time spent now will serve you well the next time you pack your bags and head for the airport.

#101 Join The Club

Whenever you arrive at the airport early or your flight is delayed, you kill time by wandering aimlessly through the terminal, browsing the airport gift shops, munching on cheap snacks, and then finally falling into a terribly uncomfortable plastic chair designed for the average kindergartner.

What's Wrong?

➤ Your wasting your time and your life.

➤ The snacks are of little nutritional value.

➤ If you actually do buy something in one of the shops, you'll have to carry it home.

➤ Your incredibly bored.

➤ The pain you get from the plastic chair will only get worse once you do get into your airline seat.

➤ You think the airline clubs are only for first class passengers.

Some Success Strategies:

If you fly a lot, join an airline club. The clubs offer free drinks, snacks, a variety of newspapers and magazines, a place to relax, plus meeting rooms. If you have work to do, you can grab a desk with a phone which also let's you plug in your computer and access the Internet or your office. Some even have hot showers! The club rooms are much more comfortable than any airport terminal and the costs are fairly reasonable. Just because you're not in first class, doesn't mean you have to travel second rate.

Summary

Travel, especially to foreign lands, can be one of the most enriching components of your job responsibility. Planning well in advance of your actual trip is the key to smooth travel. Of course, the unexpected can always happen, but good preparation can minimize the effects of some disasters along the way.

A good, effective, professional travel agent can make life on the road much easier and less costly for you, because the typical travel agent will perform these kinds of services:

- Comparison shop airlines and hotels to get the best rates

- Wait-list you for the most favorable flights and fares

- Find rooms when all hotels are booked

- Obtain refunds for services not fulfilled

- Assist you with your passport application

- Provide you with detailed information about the destinations and facilities

- Help you ensure the schedule is a realistic one

- Track your frequent flyer miles

Finally, keeping a cool head and using common sense are two of the best attributes you can demonstrate as a business traveler. Anything else is, to put things bluntly, stupid.

Additional Resources
From Richard Chang Associates, Inc.
Publications Division

Practical Guidebook Collection

Quality Improvement Series

Continuous Process Improvement

Continuous Improvement Tools, Volume 1

Continuous Improvement Tools, Volume 2

Step-By-Step Problem Solving

Meetings That Work!

Improving Through Benchmarking

Succeeding As A Self-Managed Team

Satisfying Internal Customers First!

Process Reengineering In Action

Measuring Organizational Improvement Impact

Management Skills Series

Coaching Through Effective Feedback

Expanding Leadership Impact

Mastering Change Management

On-The-Job Orientation And Training

Re-Creating Teams During Transitions

Planning Successful Employee Performance

Coaching For Peak Employee Performance

Evaluating Employee Performance

Interviewing And Selecting High Performers

High-Impact Training Series

Creating High-Impact Training

Identifying Targeted Training Needs

Mapping A Winning Training Approach

Producing High-Impact Learning Tools

Applying Successful Training Techniques

Measuring The Impact Of Training

Make Your Training Results Last

Workplace Diversity Series

Capitalizing On Workplace Diversity

Successful Staffing In A Diverse Workplace

Team Building For Diverse Work Groups

Communicating In A Diverse Workplace

Tools For Valuing Diversity

High Performance Team Series

Success Through Teamwork

Building A Dynamic Team

Measuring Team Performance

Team Decision-Making Techniques

Guidebooks are also available in fine bookstores.

ADDITIONAL RESOURCES
FROM RICHARD CHANG ASSOCIATES, INC.
PUBLICATIONS DIVISION

PERSONAL GROWTH AND DEVELOPMENT COLLECTION
Managing Your Career in a Changing Workplace
Unlocking Your Career Potential
Marketing Yourself and Your Career
Making Career Transitions

101 STUPID THINGS SERIES
101 Stupid Things Trainers Do To Sabotage Success
101 Stupid Things Supervisors Do To Sabotage Success
101 Stupid Things Salespeople Do To Sabotage Success
101 Stupid Things Business Travelers Do To Sabotage Success
101 Stupid Things Employees Do To Sabotage Success

TRAINING PRODUCTS
Step-By-Step Problem Solving TOOLKIT™
Meetings That Work! Practical Guidebook TOOLPAK™
Continuous Improvement Tools Volume 1 Practical Guidebook TOOLPAK™

PACKAGED TRAINING PROGRAMS
High Involvement Teamwork™
Continuous Process Improvement

VIDEOTAPES
Mastering Change Management**
Quality: You Don't Have To Be Sick To Get Better*
Achieving Results Through Quality Improvement*
Total Quality: Myths, Methods, Or Miracles**
Featuring Drs. Ken Blanchard and Richard Chang
Empowering The Quality Effort**
Featuring Drs. Ken Blanchard and Richard Chang
Optimizing Customer Value*
Featuring Richard Chang
Creating High-Impact Training*
Featuring Richard Chang

TOTAL QUALITY VIDEO SERIES AND WORKBOOKS
Building Commitment**
Teaming Up**
Applied Problem Solving**
Self-Directed Evaluation**

* Produced by American Media Inc.   ** Produced by Double Vision Studios

About The Publisher

Richard Chang Associates, Inc. is a diversified organizational improvement consulting firm based in Irvine, California. They provide a wide range of products and services to organizations worldwide in the areas of organizational development, quality improvement, team performance, and learning systems. The Publications Division of Richard Chang Associates, Inc., established to provide individuals with a wide variety of practical resources for continuous learning in the workplace or on a personal level, is pleased to bring you this book.

Richard Chang Associates, Inc.
Publications Division
15265 Alton Parkway, Suite 300
Irvine, CA 92618
(800) 756-8096   (949) 727-7477
Fax: (949) 727-7007
www.richardchangassociates.com